W9-AVI-730

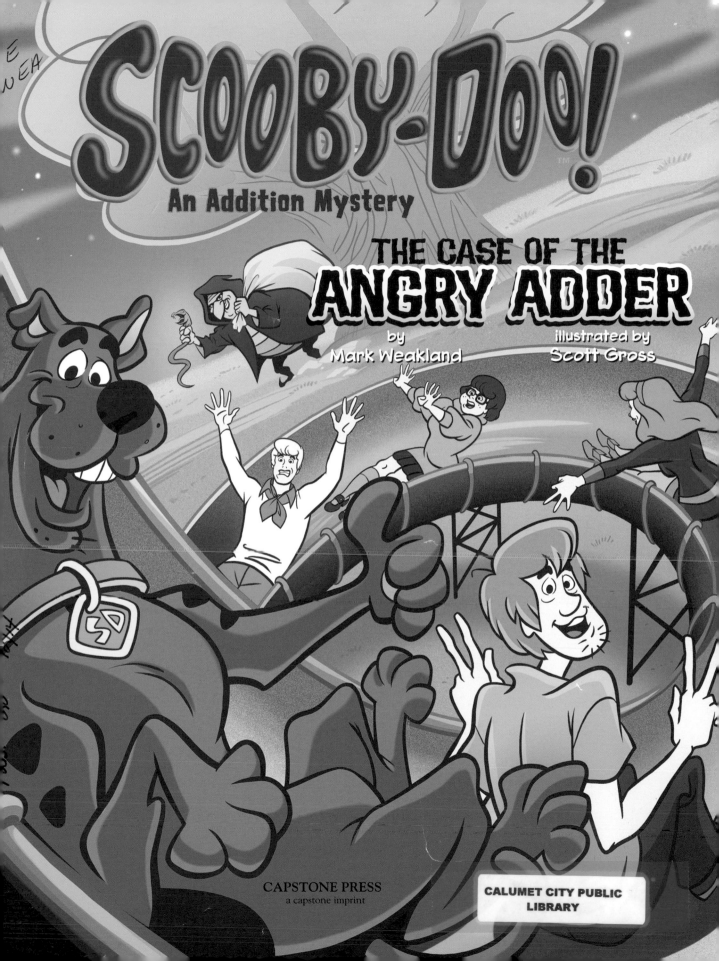

SCOOBY-DOO!

An Addition Mystery

THE CASE OF THE ANGRY ADDER

by
Mark Weakland

illustrated by
Scott Gross

CAPSTONE PRESS
a capstone imprint

Published in 2015 by Capstone Press
A Capstone Imprint
1710 Roe Crest Drive
North Mankato, Minnesota 56003
www.capstonepub.com

Library of Congress Cataloging-in-Publication Data
Weakland, Mark, author.
Scooby-Doo! an addition mystery : the case of the angry adder /
by Mark Weakland ; illustrated by Scott Gross.
pages cm.—(Solve it with Scooby-Doo! : math)
Summary: "The popular Scooby-Doo and the Mystery Inc. gang
teach kids all about addition"—Provided by publisher.
Audience: Age 5–7.
Audience: Grades K to 3.
Includes bibliographical references and index.
ISBN 978-1-4914-1539-9 (library binding)
1. Addition—Juvenile literature. 2. Snakes—Juvenile literature.
3. Scooby-Doo (Fictitious character)—Juvenile literature. I. Gross, Scott, illustrator. II. Title. III.
Title: Case of the angry adder.
QA115.W43 2015
513.2'11—dc23   2014001829

Editor: Shelly Lyons
Designer: Lori Bye
Art Director: Nathan Gassman
Production Specialist: Charmaine Whitman
The illustrations in this book were created digitally.

Thanks to our adviser for his expertise, research, and advice:
Jean B. Nganou, PhD
Department of Mathematics
University of Oregon

Printed in the United States of America in North Mankato, Minnesota.
032014   008087CGF14

Crystal Cove had a problem—a snake problem. Snakes were mysteriously appearing in the most unlikely places. Two showed up in the library. One slithered through the supermarket. One coiled in little Tyrone's sandbox. The ghost in the purple cape had struck again. Mayor Jones was not happy!

2+1+1. Put them together and you get 4. It's simple addition.

Very good, Mr. Mayor. You could also say 2+2=4.

Add the other snakes from around town, and we have a mystery on our hands!

I'm calling Scooby and the gang.

The gang was busy watching the *The Wild Animal Show*, with Guy Feral. The show had been filmed in Crystal Cove. Just then, the phone rang. Scooby-Doo and Shaggy took the call.

Rakes?

Add 5 more from this slide, and you get 15.
And there are 5 snakes here too. 5+5+5+5=20. That's 20 snakes in all. Or we can just count up by fives: 5, 10, 15, 20. That's a lot of snakes!
5 + 5 + 5 + 5 = 20

Meanwhile Scooby and Shaggy had stopped at Dave's Snack Shack.

"Our security camera got video of the ghost," said Dave. "Take a look."

$2+2+6$ $=10$

Scooby and Shaggy saw a ghost slinking through the store. It put 2 snakes on the shelves. Then the ghost added 2 snakes. Finally it added 6 more.

"2+2+6=10 snakes, Scoob," said Shaggy.

"10 rakes!" said Scooby.

"That does add up to 10!" said Dave.
"We also found this strange note."

I love ADDING to this town's problems.

Sincerely,

The Angry Adder

Dave showed the note to Scooby and Shaggy.

"Rangry Radder!" cried Scooby.

"You got that right," said Dave.

"No!" yelled Shaggy, pointing out the window. "He means he sees the Angry Adder. And he's right outside!"

Scooby and Shaggy bolted out the door. The Angry Adder turned in a swirl of purple and ran.

Stop!

Follow that creep, Scoob!

At the park, Fred, Velma, and Daphne were setting a trap. "The Adder put 10 snakes on that bench," said Fred. "We'll add 10 fake snakes here and 10 more over there," said Velma. "That's three 10s!"

10+10+10=30.

The gang hid and waited. Suddenly the Adder burst into the open. He skidded to a stop when he saw the extra snakes.

Fred pulled the rope. The net closed.

"Hey," said Dave. "It's Guy Feral, from *The Wild Animal Show!*"

"I don't like snakes, and I don't like this town," snarled Guy. "I was filming here when a snake bit my big toe! I wanted to give snakes and this town a bad name. You meddling kids and your dog stopped me!"

"Scooby and the gang solved the mystery!" said the mayor. "I'll treat you all to snacks at the Snack Shack."

Glossary

equal—being the same in number; the sign for "equal to" is =

investigate—to check to find out something

meddling—busying oneself with something that is not one's concern

mystery—something that is hard to explain or understand

security camera—a camera used in stores or homes to keep the area safe

slink—to move in a smooth, flowing way

Internet Sites

FactHound offers a safe, fun way to find Internet sites related to this book. All of the sites on FactHound have been researched by our staff.

Here's all you do:

Visit www.facthound.com

Type in this code: 9781491415399

Super-cool stuff!

Check out projects, games and lots more at
www.capstonekids.com